Free Verse Editions

Edited by Jon Thompson

remanence

Boyer Rickel

Parlor Press
West Lafayette, Indiana
www.parlorpress.com

Parlor Press LLC, West Lafayette, Indiana 47906

Printed in the United States of America
S A N: 2 5 4 - 8 8 7 9

Library of Congress Cataloging-in-Publication Data

Rickel, Boyer.
  Remanence / Boyer Rickel.
     p. cm. -- (Free verse editions)
  ISBN 978-1-60235-075-5 (pbk. : alk. paper) -- ISBN 978-1-
60235-076-2 (adobe ebook)
  1. Free verse. I. Title.
  PS3568.I35335R46 2008
  811'.54--dc22

                              2008038407

Cover photo: Morgan Schuldt. Used by permission.
Cover design: Gary Kautto and Jamey Aiken.
Author photo: Barbara Cully. Used by permission.
Printed on acid-free paper.

Parlor Press, LLC is an independent publisher of scholarly and
trade titles in print and multimedia formats. This book is available
in paper and Adobe eBook formats from Parlor Press on the World
Wide Web at http://www.parlorpress.com or through online
and brick-and-mortar bookstores. For submission information
or to find out about Parlor Press publications, write to Parlor
Press, 816 Robinson St., West Lafayette, Indiana, 47906, or e-mail
editor@parlorpress.com.

for Barbara Cully

Contents

Initial conditions. *3*

Pink stranger. *4*

Velocity. *5*

The death of anecdote. *6*

Foreboding. *7*

Longing. *8*

Forgiveness. *9*

Cold glow. *10*

Portrait. *11*

Reckoning. *12*

Shame. *13*

Glance. *14*

Allure. *15*

Face to the wall. *16*

Surface. *17*

Waiting. *18*

In the interval. *19*

Duty. *20*

Ghosting. *21*

Habitat. *22*

Born from nothingness, *23*

Temporary. *24*

Vestige. *25*

Hiddenness. *26*

Peripheral. *27*

After disaster. *28*

Residue. *29*

Terminus. *30*

Childhood. *31*

Middle distance. *32*

Blood tracer. *33*

Dispersion (dissolution). *34*

Latent. *35*

Tidal. *36*

Inexact measures. *37*

Glass houses. *38*

Breathed-on mirror. *39*

Working methods. *40*

In reserve. *41*

On he & she — *45*

On death — *46*

On setting — *47*

On I & you — *49*

On animals — *51*

On consciousness — *52*

On nostalgia — *53*

On making — *54*

On hope — *56*

Acknowledgments *57*

Note *59*

About the Author *61*

Free Verse Editions *63*

The small nouns
Crying faith

—George Oppen

remanence

remanence *n. Physics.* The magnetic
induction that remains in a material after
removal of the magnetizing force.

—*The American Heritage Dictionary*

Initial conditions.

Awakened by a herd of cows from sleeping pills that should have killed him.

Into inaccuracy.

The train, at a distance, pulling up the hill in advance of its noise.

This morning pelicans glide in formation across the glass tabletop at my side.

Corrected, slipping over the metal railing into the ocean.

Pink stranger.

Dust, what is the duty of the depths to surface?

Questions: echolocation.

The leviathan closing in on prey.

Easy, actions of the mind not subject to reality.

Resurrection a phenomenon of memory.

Velocity.

The fox who hears the water running under ice.

All cry and no occasion.

We'd watched the Santa Anas shatter wavetop after wavetop sunlight geomatrized into the color spectrum.

To have been, a poet said, even once, seems beyond undoing.

The back longs for the front, rain for sun, meat in the freezer for distant thoughts.

The death of anecdote.

Remember to show your work, we were told, when tested.

It was evening, or morning, or the middle of the night.

From an open window, irreal etudes at the height of the acacia tops—a child's keyboard efforts—shaped the rhythm of my walk.

Errors of form; the pattern of a life.

Instead, after patient looking, a face emerges incompletely from the worn surface of a fresco.

Foreboding.

Having said it, he watched it, singed and twisting, a slip of smoke dissolving in candle-light above the table.

The spaciousness inside the room of a moment.

Among the luxuries a safe life affords: imagining the worst.

The evidence, spectral, admitted before the mind's tribunal.

A tremor registers in the legs, an animal underground having shaken itself upon waking.

Longing.

"Who will wash me?" the body-washer asked her daughter, who lay on the metal table.

"From the details of extravagant, anonymous pain, a kind of pleasure," writes a critic.

I think, End of the road?

On either side of the corpus callosum, a separate awareness.

In the morning, the black-winged angel chalked on the brickwork of the library plaza is hosed away by a city workman.

Forgiveness.

The problem of infinities.

Spanning the beach, decayed gradations, one gull so freshly dead it seemed a toe might nudge it into flight, the next a dreary hump, mere moldered feathers, and then a heap of bones, a necklace cast aside with one long golden pendant, and so on.

A ladder, each rung the future of the rung below, until nothing.

A buoyant emptiness.

The smell of just-sprayed sidewalks before the start of business.

Cold glow.

A missing muscle in *David*'s upper back—his body's only imperfection—from a defect in the block of granite Michelangelo chose to work with.

The underneath of promise.

Because it's the abstract we can agree upon, the pursuit of the real, made of particulars—impossible.

Idea as chemical action in the brain, the self erased.

The water black with the ink of words from books the invaders threw into the river at the sacking of the city.

Portrait.

On the head of a pin, the artist used a single hair, each stroke applied between the beats of his heart.

A face shivers on the surface of a pan of water.

Since in us is where the dead exist.

The rational having set a place for transcendence.

Both doors open.

Reckoning.

Blowing notes above the din of rush-hour traffic, a man with a horn on a bridge.

Like making love to reweave the frayed lace intricacies of a lie.

"Is it my job to know you?"

Lucretius noted the sweetness, as a storm approached, of watching from shore the peril of others at sea.

The skin beneath the peeled strip of bark dried slick, though the bark, slow-closing curtains, over many years grew back.

Shame.

Wrapped in newspaper, behind a brick in the chimney, a canary inside a frayed blue purse inside a can.

A continual performance.

Love igniting that place in the caudate nucleus.

The day so searing, when walking from sunlight into the shade of a palo verde, I felt the cool glide up my shins as though I'd stepped into a pool of water.

The ghost had died, returning as a body.

14

Glance.

Incomplete immediacy.

Inside one's body, an absence documented.

Having laid the cello on the bed at their insistence, Casals grew ill when the soldiers touched it.

The pleasure—pressure—of a surface.

Through the trees it might have been a pond, though we were in a hurry to return before darkness.

Allure.

Breathing in, one can't speak.

Instead of words, he stirred the tea leaves at the bottom of the cup into flight.

The future that dwells in us without our knowing.

Standing before the intricate pastel tapestries, I tried to picture their brightly colored backs, protected from the light five hundred years by linen linings.

The room lit faintly by the bluish glow up from the ocean.

Face to the wall.

I read into the mention of your trip to Rome next winter a refusal.

The package mailed.

A portion of the future, measured in the mind, containing an arrival.

Am I the guest who doesn't plan to leave?

A long stone placed upright on the ground, says the essayist, becomes a presence: a dialogue begins.

Surface.

The painter recalled his childhood through his skin: "small cold rooms lit by hot flashes of anger."

Mornings in bed, the pulse of your breath on my neck.

The dunes marked here and there by swallows' shadows as by blown bits of paper.

Will the dead, as we crowd the earth, resist the urge to visit?

The survivor said they washed themselves with ash, or sand.

Waiting.

The snake brain hums the background tone of one's being, reports the neurologist.

A kind of island.

Lit by moonlight, the lines of wave froth zippered up and down the shore.

We move from gifts to coins, so you lock the bedroom door behind me.

The face the only place where muscles connect directly to the skin.

In the interval.

A feeling's duration, the decay of a note struck at the keyboard.

Candles melt into pools on the mantle.

The forms—signs—sheets draping our bodies make.

The simultaneous search for pain and its relief.

Two kinds of strangeness, a word and a word (lovers?), alongside one another.

Duty.

A stocky yellow dog yapped and paced the shore, waiting for his boy to emerge from the water.

Do we deny our dead the comfort of oblivion by sounding their names?

(One can even see the body in an echo.)

Things, empty of ideas, wait to be used—a chair, its shadow on the lawn.

As though one could resist the tug of the mind's idle energy.

Ghosting.

The animal within, an awakening encumbrance.

Your voice the sound of leaves falling onto leaves.

It made me laugh that someone had mistakenly dusted it away—in a museum, carved by a master, an ivory figure of the tyrant no larger than a speck.

Taped to the refrigerator door, charcoal rubbings of common objects: a key, a comb, three large foreign coins.

Our moods, still pools—anger or tenderness—wait for any random ruffling, a waterbug, the wrinkling of a breeze, to ignite a fist or initiate caresses.

Habitat.

He heard inside himself the scream of a horse.

Blown neurons, fragments of death.

And sleep, the fully furnished house we maintain that empties upon waking.

When I imagine you do not exist, I make and unmake you, all at once.

A brittle flycasing, trembling in the web.

Born from nothingness,

all artistic practice, the sculptor claimed, culminates in another form of nothingness, which is everything.

The space that is left after peeling the sphere's surface.

From an accidental ink mark on the white silk duvet, you formed the word "love" in tiny blue letters.

The reattached hand transforming from porcelain to pink.

No matter what I sang into the tidal din, every note contained in the breaking waves, I heard the song's harmonic accompaniment.

Temporary.

The desperate will consider a boat made of ice.

The one in love, the fool, for whom the boundaries have disappeared.

The teacup spoke, the chair, the brass doorknob, the child ascribing consciousness to every object in the room.

You feel as though you play the role of nothing, that you fail to show up for your own life.

Having seen the stars once (the clouds closing over), the old man sailed (what else could he do?) as though he knew the coordinates.

Vestige.

Such pleasure we shared, though on waking, like something overheard at a cafe table.

A sentence underlined in a book you'll never reopen.

One said, "like lace," then "ghosts"; the other, "fingers, or rivulets"—of the fine white sand that blew across the mica-blackened beach.

The scrim effacing memory.

The partial shedding of our bodies when at the movies.

Hiddenness.

The loved one not in love—you imagine how easily and with what grace he undertakes his daily tasks.

The idea of a room opening up inside one's body.

A rhythmic knock and no one there but the sudden flutter of a woodpecker and a dime-size hole on the porch's fascia.

When we think we know, do we alter reality?

Lightening struck, the people caught fire, then the tarp collapsed extinguishing them.

Peripheral.

The eyes of fish laid out on beds of ice in the market.

When will this wick of fear burn off?, I wonder.

The air suddenly chill.

In the morning, he found that the giant spiral of wheel ruts in the vacant lot had filled with rain.

"The silence of outer space never seemed so loud," the singer said of the death of his hero.

After disaster.

Chance governed, our concerns focused onto a single point.

Your argument now with punctuation, commas, dashes, since word as ash, word as dust blown every which way, coats the streets.

A face containing many other faces—is it no one?

The child, given paper and crayons, drew a series of angels, speculations on the nature of eternity.

The brain's economy: one object, one neuron.

Residue.

So desire is the urge produced by a question mark?

He watched two sun-darkened men toss aside their boards and, boisterous as boys, wrestle in the surf, each determined to throw the other headfirst into the breaking waves.

One small part of what I do not know.

Wind enough you could hear the whistling of telephone wires.

Melancholy an engine of making.

Terminus.

Before the larval parasite killed the spider, the spider spun a platform on which its guest could develop into a wasp.

Were we supposed to think the ghost in the episode was real, or merely a projection of the hero's longing?

The mind made of words.

The water rose and finally the pounding stopped.

How often in a loved one's face you awaken in ruin.

Childhood.

An eternity, recollected.

How long had he been waiting for the twitch at the end of the line?

First sleep of a night.

A thudding—concrete walls falling in a vast underground room.

The photographer called freaks "aristocrats," born already with their trauma, not needing, as we do, to discover it.

Middle distance.

The way he shook his head, who could tell if he confirmed or denied the assertion.

Because the past stands not behind but in front of us.

Where lovers meet.

"Drift, wait, obey," words the songwriter clipped and taped to the wall at his desk.

The cardinal in the palo verde looked at me as though it had once known language.

Blood tracer.

Are we just matter dreaming?

The form, ambiguous, on the half-lit shore, worked on his senses until it leaked into a fact.

Whose specimen am I?

Now you beat the drum, now you stop.

On the battlefield, small blue phosphorous flames flickered around the corpses.

Dispersion (dissolution).

Blown sand: the data of memory.

Her degradation, graceful as . . .

So today's not the day after all.

Words not of the prophet, but of the prophet's companion.

The room's thick carpets, which made me draw back for fear of electric shock.

Latent.

The jacket was warm and smelled of cologne.

On a calendar, the box of each day a door left ajar.

A stranger's marginalia in the library book.

Of the Picasso painting, the Alzheimer's patient said, "He's trying to tell a story with words that don't exist."

The scale of the news fit my mood: mice too sing for love.

Tidal.

Two girls in matching blue plaid skirts and white blouses collected for the victims.

All that matters most surpassing reason.

Conveyed by the hiss of sudden rain.

You made of the meal a ceremony of reconciliation.

The master's highest goal a pure nothing.

Inexact measures.

But his eyes moved, conducting the silence.

The ocean in the distance.

A dance inspired by doom-eager friends.

What else are we to do with time?

Desire, difficulty; darkness: an absence; defects a necessity.

Glass houses.

"I was a bit like paint or plaster—living matter, that which allowed him to create," said the model.

And what does this word suffering taste of?

The survivor said she'd escaped death only to discover she was no longer alive.

Streets with their knowable ends; roads inviting us to leave.

Your change of tone a shock, like missing a step.

Breathed-on mirror.

Listening to the musical passage, no words for what I thought I understood.

Steam off the lake.

A habit of calm.

An image taken from the past to give what's temporary—this moment—a memorable face.

The prisoner, not permitted to attend, had a scene of the funeral tattooed on his back.

Working methods.

Yours was the face I imagined before I knew the name.

Some incomplete idea of fact.

On morning walks, a neighborhood of unseen sleepers, lives blooming in the dreams of a hundred houses.

When the sea boiled, the fisherman's first guess was a ghost.

At the margin of the already known, where discovery happens.

In reserve.

The iceberg sang—the pressure of water rushing through a crevasse.

The old woman's sensation of speed as the children chased the ball.

That words are oxygen.

That ideas detonate in slow motion.

He felt an inward (fugitive?) turning as he read the novel.

On he & she —

Awakened by a herd of cows from sleeping pills that should have killed him.

Having said it, he watched it, singed and twisting, a slip of smoke dissolving in candle-light above the table. Instead of words, he stirred the tea leaves at the bottom of the cup into flight. He heard inside himself the scream of a horse. The one in love, the fool, for whom the boundaries have disappeared.

In the morning, he found that the giant spiral of wheel ruts in the vacant lot had filled with rain. He watched two sun-darkened men toss aside their boards and, boisterous as boys, wrestle in the surf, each determined to throw the other headfirst into the breaking waves. How long had he been waiting for the twitch at the end of the line?

The way he shook his head, who could tell if he confirmed or denied the assertion. The form, ambiguous, on the half-lit shore, worked on his senses until it leaked into a fact. But his eyes moved, conducting the silence. He felt an inward (fugitive?) turning as he read the novel.

———

"Who will wash me?" the body-washer asked her daughter, who lay on the metal table. Her degradation, graceful as . . .

Two girls in matching blue plaid skirts and white blouses collected for the victims. The survivor said she'd escaped death only to discover she was no longer alive. The old woman's sensation of speed as the children chased the ball.

On death —

Into inaccuracy. Questions: echolocation. All cry and no occasion.

To have been, a poet said, even once, seems beyond undoing. The spaciousness inside the room of a moment. The problem of infinities. A buoyant emptiness.

Since in us is where the dead exist. Both doors open. A continual performance.

The ghost had died, returning as a body. Incomplete immediacy. The pleasure—pressure—of a surface. Breathing in, one can't speak.

Will the dead, as we crowd the earth, resist the urge to visit? Do we deny our dead the comfort of oblivion by sounding their names? (One can even see the body in an echo.)

The space that is left after peeling the sphere's surface. A sentence underlined in a book you'll never reopen. Desire, difficulty; darkness: an absence; defects a necessity. And what does this word suffering taste of? A habit of calm. Some incomplete idea of fact. That words are oxygen.

On setting —

The train, at a distance, pulling up the hill in advance of its noise. Corrected, slipping over the metal railing into the ocean. It was evening, or morning, or the middle of the night.

Dust, what is the duty of depths to surface? In the morning, the black-winged angel chalked on the brickwork of the library plaza is hosed away by a city workman. The smell of just-sprayed sidewalks before the start of business. The water black with the ink of words from books the invaders threw into the river at the sacking of the city. Blowing notes above the din of rush-hour traffic, a man with a horn on a bridge.

The skin beneath the peeled strip of bark dried slick, though the bark, slow-closing curtains, over many years grew back. Wrapped in newspaper, behind a brick in the chimney, a canary inside a frayed blue purse inside a can. Having laid the cello on the bed at their insistence, Casals grew ill when the soldiers touched it.

The room lit faintly by the bluish glow up from the ocean. The package mailed. A kind of island. Lit by moonlight, the lines of wave froth zippered up and down the shore.

Candles melt into pools on the mantle. Things, empty of ideas, wait to be used—a chair, its shadow on the lawn. Taped to the refrigerator door, charcoal rubbings of common objects: a key, a comb, three large foreign coins. One said, "like lace," then "ghosts"; the other, "fingers, or rivulets"— of the fine white sand that blew across the mica-blackened beach.

Lightening struck, the people caught fire, then the tarp collapsed extinguishing them. The air suddenly chill. Wind enough you could hear the whistling of telephone wires. The water rose and finally the pounding stopped. A thudding— concrete walls falling in a vast underground room.

On the battlefront, small blue phosphorous flames flickered around the corpses. The jacket was warm and smelled of cologne. A stranger's marginalia in a library book. Conveyed by the hiss of sudden rain. The ocean in the distance. Streets with their knowable ends; roads inviting us to leave. Steam off the lake. The iceberg sang—the pressure of water rushing through a crevasse.

On I & you —

This morning pelicans glide in formation across the glass tabletop at my side. We'd watched the Santa Anas shatter wavetop after wavetop sunlight geomatrized into the color spectrum.

I thought, End of the road? Is it my job to know you? The day so searing, when walking from sunlight into the shade of a palo verde, I felt the cool glide up my shins as though I'd stepped into a pool of water. Through the trees it might have been a pond, though we were in a hurry to return before darkness.

Standing before the intricate pastel tapestries, I tried to picture their brightly colored backs, protected from the light five hundred years by linen linings. I read in the mention of your trip to Rome next winter a refusal. Am I the guest who doesn't plan to leave? Mornings in bed, the pulse of your breath on my neck. We move from gifts to coins, so you lock the bedroom door behind me. Two kinds of strangeness, a word and a word (lovers?), alongside one another. The forms—signs—sheets draping our bodies make. Your voice the sound of leaves falling on leaves.

It made me laugh that someone had mistakenly dusted it away—in a museum, carved by a master, an ivory figure of the tyrant no larger than a speck. Our moods, still pools—anger or tenderness—wait for any random ruffling, a waterbug, the wrinkling breeze, to ignite a fist or initiate caresses. And sleep, the fully furnished house we maintain that empties upon waking. When I imagine you do not exist, I make and unmake you, all at once. From an accidental ink mark on the white silk duvet, you formed the word "love" in tiny blue letters.

No matter what I sang into the tidal din, every note contained in the breaking waves, I heard the song's harmonic accompaniment. Such pleasures we shared, though on waking, like something overheard at a café table. The partial shedding of our bodies when at the movies. When will this wick of fear burn off?, I wonder. Chance governed, our concerns focused onto a single point. Your argument now with punctuation, commas, dashes, since word as ash, word as dust blown every which way, coats the streets. One small part of what I do not know. Because the past stands not behind but in front of us.

The cardinal in the palo verde looked at me as thought it had once known language. Are we just matter dreaming? Whose specimen am I? Now you beat the drum, now you stop. The room's thick carpets, which made me draw back for fear of electric shock. The scale of the news fit my mood: mice too sing for love. You made of the meal a ceremony of reconciliation. Your change of tone a shock, like missing a step. Listening to the musical passage, no words for what I thought I understood. Yours was the face I imagined before I knew the name.

On animals —

The leviathan closing in on prey. The fox who hears the water running under ice. A tremor registers in the legs, an animal underground having shaken itself upon waking.

Spanning the beach, decayed gradations, one gull so freshly dead it seemed a toe might nudge it into flight, the next a dreary hump, mere moldered feathers, and then a heap of bones, a necklace cast aside with one long golden pendant, and so on. The dunes marked here and there by swallows' shadows as by blown bits of paper. A stocky yellow dog yapped and paced the shore, waiting for his boy to emerge from the water.

The animal within, an awakening encumbrance. A brittle flycasing, trembling in the web. The eyes of fish laid out on beds of ice in the market.

On consciousness —

Easy, actions of the mind not subject to reality. Among the luxuries a safe life affords: imagining the worst. The evidence, spectral, admitted before the mind's tribunal. On either side of the corpus callosum, a separate awareness. Idea as chemical action in the brain, the self erased. The rational having set a place for transcendence. Love igniting that place in the caudate nucleus.

Inside one's body, an absence documented. A portion of the future, measured in the mind, containing an arrival. The simultaneous search for pain and its relief. As though one could resist the tug of the mind's idle energy.

Blown neurons, fragments of death. You feel as though you play the role of nothing, that you fail to show up for your own life. The idea of a room opening up inside one's body. When we think we know, do we alter reality?

The brain's economy: one object, one neuron. The mind made of words. All that matters most surpassing reason. At the margin of the already known, where discovery happens. That ideas detonate in slow motion.

On nostalgia —

Instead, after patient looking, a face emerges incompletely from the worn surface of a fresco. Resurrection a phenomenon of memory. Remember to show your work, we were told, when tested. A ladder, each rung the future of the rung below, until nothing.

A face shivers on the surface of a pan of water. The future that dwells in us without our knowing. The scrim effacing memory. An eternity, recollected.

A face containing many other faces—is it no one? Blown sand: the data of memory. How often in a loved one's face you awaken in ruin. An image taken from the past to give what's temporary—this moment—a memorable face.

On making—

The back longs for the front, rain for sun, meat in the freezer for distant thoughts. From an open window, irreal etudes at the height of the acacia tops—a child's keyboard efforts—shaped the rhythm of my walk.

Errors of form; the pattern of a life. "From the details of extravagant, anonymous pain, a kind of pleasure," writes a critic. A missing muscle in *David*'s upper back—his body's only imperfection—from a defect in the block of granite Michelangelo chose to work with. Because it's the abstract we can agree upon, the pursuit of the real, made of particulars—impossible.

On the head of a pin, the artist used a single hair, each stroke applied between the beats of his heart. A long stone placed upright on the ground, says the essayist, becomes a presence: a dialogue begins.

The painter recalled his childhood through his skin: "small cold rooms lit by hot flashes of anger." The snake brain hums the background tone of one's being, reports the neurologist. The face the only place where muscles connect directly to the skin. A feeling's duration, the decay of a note struck at the keyboard. The reattached hand transforming from porcelain to pink.

All artistic practice, the sculptor claimed, culminates in another form of nothingness, which is everything. The teacup spoke, the chair, the brass doorknob, the child ascribing consciousness to every object in the room. A rhythmic knock and no one there but the sudden flutter of a woodpecker and a dime-size hole on the porch's fascia.

"The silence of outer space never seemed so loud," the singer said of the death of his hero. The child, given paper and crayons, drew a series of angels, speculations on the nature of eternity. Before the larval parasite killed the spider, the spider spun a platform on which its guest could develop into a wasp.

The photographer called freaks "aristocrats," born already with their trauma, not needing, as we do, to discover it. "Drift, wait, obey," words the songwriter clipped and taped to the wall at his desk. Words not of the prophet, but of the prophet's companion. Of the Picasso painting, the Alzheimer's patient said, "He's trying to tell a story with words that don't exist." The master's highest goal a pure nothing. What else was there to do with time?

"I was a bit like paint or plaster—living matter, that which allowed him to create," said the model. The prisoner, not permitted to attend, had a scene of the funeral tattooed on his back. On morning walks, a neighborhood of unseen sleepers, lives blooming in the dreams of a hundred houses.

On hope —

The underneath of promise. Like making love to reweave the frayed lace intricacies of a lie.

Lucretius noted the sweetness, as a storm approached, of watching from shore the peril of others at sea. The survivor said they washed themselves with ash, or sand. Having seen the stars once (the clouds closing over), the old man sailed (what else could he do?) as though he knew the coordinates.

The desperate will consider a boat made of ice. The loved one not in love—you imagine how easily and with what grace he undertakes his daily tasks. So desire is the urge produced by a question mark? Melancholy an engine of making.

Were we supposed to think the ghost in the episode was real, or merely a projection of the hero's longing?

First sleep of a night. Where lovers meet. So today's not the day after all. On a calendar, the box of each day a door left ajar. A dance inspired by doom-eager friends.

When the sea boiled, the fisherman's first guess was a ghost.

Acknowledgments

Many thanks to the editors of the following journals who first published these poems:

Antennae: "Dispersion (dissolution).," "Face to the wall.," "Latent.," "Longing.," part two of "On he & she—," "Pink stranger.";
CUE: "On consciousness—," "On making—";
Free Verse: "Cold glow.," "Surface.," "The death of anecdote.";
NOON (Journal of the Short Poem): "Foreboding.," "Forgive-ness.," "Shame.";
No Tell Motel: "After disaster.," "Childhood.," "Habitat.," "Pe-ripheral.," "Vestige.";
Seneca Review: "Glance.";
Sonora Review: "On animals—," "On setting—," "Residue.," "Terminus.";
Tight: "Glass houses.," "Initial conditions.," "Portrait.," "Tem-porary.," "Waiting."

My thanks to Morgan Schuldt and Barbara Cully, in whose fellowship *remanence* was written, and Mike and Carole Marks for their generous support. I'd also like to thank The National Endowment for the Arts and The Arizona Commission on the Arts for their support, which gave me time and hope.

Note

The material of *remanence* in part derives from quoted, paraphrased, alchemized, or misprisioned language of Diane Arbus, Francis Bacon, John Berger, Charles Bernstein, Elizabeth Bishop, Italo Calvino, Anne Carson, Paul Celan, Hart Crane, Willem deKooning, Emily Dickinson, Geoff Dyer, Bob Dylan, Jack Gilbert, Jean Helion, Jane Hirshfield, the *I Ching*, James Longenbach, Michael Mason, Ian McEwan, Montaigne, Jorge Orteiza, Alicia Ostriker, Marcel Proust, R. M. Rilke, Peter Schjeldahl, W. G. Sebald, and Christian Wiman.

About the Author

Boyer Rickel's books include *arreboles* (Wesleyan) and *Taboo*, essays (Wisconsin). Recipient of poetry fellowships from the NEA and Arizona Commission on the Arts, his poems and nonfiction have appeared in more than sixty print and online journals and anthologies. Since 1991 he has taught in the University of Arizona Creative Writing Program.

Photograph of the author by Barbara Cully. Used by permission.

Free Verse Editions

Edited by Jon Thompson

2008

Quarry by Carolyn Guinzio
Between the Twilight and the Sky by Jennie Neighbors
The Prison Poems by Miguel Hernández,
    translated by Michael Smith
remanence by Boyer Rickel
What Stillness Illuminated by Yermiyahu Ahron Taub

2007

Child in the Road by Cindy Savett
Verge by Morgan Lucas Schuldt
The Flying House by Dawn-Michelle Baude

2006

Physis by Nicolas Pesque, translated by Cole Swensen
Puppet Wardrobe by Daniel Tiffany
These Beautiful Limits by Thomas Lisk
The Wash by Adam Clay

2005

A Map of Faring by Peter Riley
Signs Following by Ger Killeen
Winter Journey [Viaggio d'inverno] by Attilio Bertolucci,
    translated by Nicholas Benson

www.ingramcontent.com/pod-product-compliance
Lightning Source LLC
Chambersburg PA
CBHW032029090426
42741CB00006B/788